ALEX RODRIGUEZ

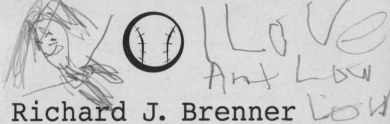

Richard J. Brenner

SCHOLASTIC INC.

New York Toronto London Auckland Sydney
Mexico City New Delhi Hong Kong Buenos Aires

This book is dedicated to Dr. Johnson,
with great love and appreciation for all that you have done
for me during the writing of this book.

I also dedicate this book to all my readers, who I hope will enjoy this
biography. I also hope that they will consider the fact that very few people ever get
to play professional ball, but that the pursuit of excellence, in school and in
whatever else interests them, is a very worthy goal. In the big scheme of life,
in fact, being able to hit a round ball with a long stick is probably not as important
as doing research on finding a cure for cancer, preventing global
warming, or striving for tolerance, equal justice, and world peace.

With great thanks and appreciation to everybody whose time and talents have contributed
to this book, including John Douglas, who is always graceful, even in the
most trying of circumstances; Jean Cohn, who has risen to the challenge, and Marilyn,
who is always there for me, selflessly doing whatever needs to be done.

BOOK DESIGN AND LAYOUT: **Jean Cohn**
COPY EDITOR: **John Douglas**
PROOF READER AND RESEARCHER: **Marilyn**

PHOTO CREDITS:
SportsChrome supplied the cover photo and all interior photographs,
and **Rob Tringali** took all the pictures, with the exception of the first interior
photograph, which was taken by **Michael Zito.**

ISBN 0-439-70272-0

12 11 10 9 8 7 6 5 4 3 2 1   5 6 7 8 9 10/0

Printed in the U.S.A   40

First Scholastic printing, April 2005

AUTHOR'S NOTE: For many years, Native American groups have been appealing to sports teams not
to use the names and logos that many Native Americans find offensive, such as *Braves*, or the laugh-
ing cartoon Indian on the uniform of the Cleveland baseball team.

Out of respect for and in support of those appeals, I have chosen not to use those names in this book.
I urge all readers who agree with my position to write to the offending teams and Bud Selig, the
Commissioner of Major League Baseball, to protest the use of those names and logos.

This book was not authorized by Alex Rodriguez or Major League Baseball.

CONTENTS

ONE

THE EARLY YEARS:
Bittersweet

Alexander Emmanuel Rodriguez was born July 27, 1975, in Washington Heights, a neighborhood nestled into the northern part of Manhattan. It's a district with a rich history of being home to a succession of immigrant groups, pioneers and refugees, come to the United States from the far corners of the globe in search of a better life, seeking opportunities that had not been available to them in the countries which they had left behind.

Alex's parents, Lourdes and Victor, had come to New York from the Dominican Republic, a Caribbean country that occupies the eastern two thirds of Hispaniola, the island it shares with Haiti. The Dominican Republic is a Spanish-speaking nation that is located only 670 miles southeast of Florida, but a whole world away from the Sunshine State in terms of its meager economic development and the opportunities that are available to most of its struggling people.

The country has suffered from severe poverty throughout its history. But it has also, curiously, produced an uncommon number of baseball stars for its relatively small population, including Sammy Sosa, Alfonso Soriano, Miguel Tejada, Pedro Martinez, David Ortiz, Vladimir Guerrero, and Albert Pujols.

"Always follow your dreams, don't let anyone tell you that you can't be something."

Although Victor came from an educated and respected family, he and Lourdes still chose to come to America to make their mark. Victor was an accountant by trade, and he and Lourdes worked hard, and eventually saved enough money to buy a shoe store. Victor put in long hours to build the shop into a thriving and prosperous business. His hard work and good business practices proved so successful, that in 1979, when Alex was 4 years old, Victor was able to sell the store, and move back to the Dominican Republic with his family, which included Alex's older brother, Joe, and older sister, Susy.

The family stayed in the Caribbean country for four years, and it was during this time that Victor, who had been a catcher and first baseman in a Dominican pro league, began to teach the game of baseball to his young son.

"He was the one who taught me how to play baseball," remembered Alex. "He spoiled me, because I was the baby of the family. Back then, I always wanted to be like my dad."

"In the DR, playing ball was tougher than in America. No one had anything. In the U.S., kids have $200.00 gloves and play on fields that are like paradise. But in the DR, the fields are filled with rocks, and some kids play with cut-out milk cartons on their hands, because they can't afford to buy a mitt."

Despite the less–than–perfect conditions, Alex took to the sport quickly, and was soon playing with older children, and holding his own against nine- and ten-year-olds when he was still only six.

"I'm a terrible singer. I feel lucky to be able play baseball. You can't be gifted in everything."

"He was very focused from the time he was a young child, and he just wasn't interested in anything else, except baseball," said Lourdes. "He didn't care if it was sunny or raining, he just had to play ball, and would cry if I didn't take him to the park every day."

Alex also liked the fact that he was able to live close to many of his relatives. He was constantly surrounded by cousins, grandparents, and aunts and uncles.

In 1983, however, four years after retiring and resettling his family in the Dominican Republic, Victor moved them back to the United States.

"Sometimes parents gets kicked down by

life," explained Alex, his voice a mixture of wisdom and sympathy. "It happened to my parents when I was eight. They told me we'd move back to the Dominican in a few months, but we never did. I took it in stride."

The family settled in Kendall, Florida, a suburban Miami community, which is on the western edge of the Florida Everglades. Victor quickly opened up a shoe store in Miami, where he hoped to duplicate the success he had had in New York. But after a year, Victor decided that he wanted to move again, this time back to New York City. Lourdes, however, decided that she and the kids had moved around enough and refused to pack up and transplant herself and the children again.

After failing to persuade his wife to move back to New York, Victor walked out on her and their three children, without ever saying a word to Alex, who was nine years old. One day, he just left, as though he was going to buy a container of milk, or take a business trip, and he never came back, or even called his son, until many painful years had passed.

"I didn't know what was going on," recalled Alex. "I thought he was coming back. I thought he had gone to the store, or something."

"*Be respectful. Treat people the way you want to be treated. Respect the lowest rank and the highest rank and you'll never get in trouble.*"

Although Lourdes told her two older children that their father had left for good, she didn't have the courage to face her nine-year-old son with that harsh truth; so, for many months, Alex kept thinking that, at any moment, his father would walk through the front door of their home.

"But he never came back," said Alex, the memory flashing like sad movies in his moist green eyes. "I kept thinking that my father would come back, but he never did."

When Victor walked out of his family's life, he took away one of the two pillars upon whom Alex was constructing his emotional well-being, and he also left Lourdes, the other pillar, and her three children, in a dire financial crunch. In order to provide for her children, Lourdes was forced into working two jobs, as a secretary during the day, and as a waitress at night, dependent upon tips to put food on their table and clothes on their backs. On most nights, when Lourdes came home from her job as a waitress, Alex would be waiting up, ready to count the day's haul.

"I consider my mom to be my MVP—Most Valuable Parent," said Alex, a smile curling around his lips. "All the love I had for him I just gave to my mother. She deserved it. She's one of my best friends.

"It was hard," he continued, a slight tremor in his voice indicating just how difficult it had been for him. "I did my best to help out around the house and bring home good grades to make my mom proud."

Victor had taken a great deal away from his family, but, however unintentionally, he had also supplied Alex with an athlete's DNA, and located him in a warm environment, where Alex could play baseball 52 weeks of the year. It's even possible that Alex had learned to love the game because of his father's early instruction, and that his drive to achieve excellence in baseball was a young boy's way of trying to please and outperform his absent father.

"I used to sit at the kitchen table and count the bills and coins my mother brought home from her tips. Fifty dollars was a good night."

But, what is entirely beyond speculation is the fact that Victor's departure and desertion left a scar that has never fully healed.

"I tried to tell myself it didn't matter, but I was just lying to myself," recalled Alex. "When I was alone, I often cried. Where was my father? To this day, I don't really know how a man could do that—turn his back on his family."

After Victor had slipped silently out of his life, Alex was fortunate to find other men who would provide the kindness and guidance that would help him to stay on an even keel, and partially fill the aching void that his father's absence had created.

"I felt I always had good male leadership and mentorship around me," explained Alex. "I try not to focus on what's missing, I prefer to look at the glass as half full."

Eddie Rodriguez, a former minor league player, who is the director of the Hank Kline Boys and Girls Club in Miami, was one of the men who helped Alex, both as a coach and as someone he could talk to. After all this time, Alex still goes to the club's field in the off-season to take batting practice and field grounders, and he still considers Rodriguez to be the biggest influence on his life.

"Off the field, it's Eddie Rodriguez," said Alex, who has donated nearly two million dollars to the facility. "I've been with him at the Boys and Girls Club since I was 8 years old. Now, I'm 29, and 21 years later, he's still hitting me ground balls. He's been a good mentor and friend."

Rodriguez, who isn't related to Alex, had

tutored a number of young boys who went on to become major league stars, including Rafael Palmeiro, who has so far slugged 551 home runs, and who would become one of Alex's teammates on the Texas Rangers, and Jose Canseco, who, in 1988, became the first player ever to hit 40 home runs and steal 40 bases in the same season.

"Anyone can forget about talent, but if you're a good person, your name will be remembered a long time."

"Alex was special," recalled Rodriguez. "I don't mean that I knew he was going to be a major-leaguer the first time I saw him. You never know that when they're eight years old. All you could tell then was that he had talent, and that he was never afraid to work hard and do things the right way.

"We've had a lot of players come through the club, but nobody who has ever come through our doors ever worked harder than Alex."

Juan Arteaga, the father of Alex's boyhood best friend, A.J. Arteaga, was another adult who took an interest in Alex. Juan Arteaga helped him to develop his skills as a young player, and treated him like a second son.

"Mr. Arteaga and Eddie Rodriguez guided me and gave me their most precious gift—time," recalled Alex. "I made sure that I didn't do anything stupid to let them down."

Alex and A.J. had met one day while Alex was watching A.J. practice baseball in a neighborhood park. Juan Arteaga, who was coaching the team, spotted Alex, watching the boys play, like a hungry kid with his nose pressed against a bakery window, and asked him if he wanted to join in. Even though Alex was younger than most of the other players, he was able to step in and play up to their level.

Soon, he and A.J., who lived two blocks away from Alex, had become best friends, and Juan Arteaga had taken Alex under his wing. When he took A.J. to a ball game, he would also invite Alex, and sometimes he would buy

Alex the equipment he needed to play. Although Arteaga had seen lots of good baseball players, including his son, he told A.J. that Alex was the best player he'd ever seen.

"*We have a responsibility not just as athletes, but as members of society to treat people well. To do things the right way.*"

"Alex was only 11, and I thought my dad was crazy. How could he think that an 11-year-old kid was the best player he had ever seen? But now, I have to say that my father was a pretty good scout."

Alex's athletic role models were always players who worked hard and who, by their examples, demonstrated what it meant to be a dedicated professional, while also projecting positive personal values and good sportsmanship.

"My mom always said, 'I don't care if you turn out to be a terrible player, I just want you to be a good person,'" explained Alex. "That's the most important thing to me. Like Cal or Dale Murphy, I want people to look at me and say, 'He's a good person.'"

He was a big fan of basketball superstar Michael Jordan, who became the best player in the game, not simply because of his enormous talent, but because of how willingly and diligently he worked to develop his skills in the off-season and during practice sessions.

"I've always enjoyed practice more than playing games," explained Alex. "Practice to me is where you hone your craft. I have a great passion for constantly trying to improve."

His favorite baseball players were Atlanta center fielder, Dale Murphy; Keith Hernandez, the slick-fielding, clutch-hitting first baseman who played for the St. Louis Cardinals, before joining the New York Mets; and Cal Ripken, Jr., the indomitable shortstop of the Baltimore Orioles, who played in a record-setting 2,632 consecutive games.

"Cal Ripken was the only shortstop I knew of who hit third in the lineup, the spot where most teams put their best hitter," said Alex. "And he was also a Gold Glove fielder.

That's the type of player that I wanted to be."

Although Eddie Rodriguez had been the earliest coach to notice how hard Alex was willing to work to increase his skill level, he was just the first in an unbroken line to attest to the determination and preparation with which Alex has always approached his athletic pursuits.

"What I've learned from Cal is to respect the game, respect the fans. Nothing fancy out there. Just do your job."

"While the other boys would be sleeping, I'd find Alex doing crunches and sit-ups at seven in the morning," recalled Tony Quesada, one of the coaches on the traveling teams which Alex played for when he was in junior high school. "Even then, you would see that he had that special spark, the inner drive to perfect his skills."

Even after he'd played a night game, Alex would still want to practice, even though the lights had been turned off.

"The park guys would turn out the lights

after games and want to go home, and Alex would still want people to hit him ground balls in the dark," recalled James Colzie II, a former teammate.

And practice couldn't start early enough in the morning for Alex, who would recruit friends to hit grounders to him for an hour, starting at 6:30 in the morning, before school started.

"They thought I was a lunatic," said Alex. "After three months I ran out of friends to hit to me. It finally had to stop because school officials said I was getting too sweaty and smelly before class."

Although Alex has always been too active to become a couch potato and has never spent much time trolling the tube, he did make a point of watching a lot of baseball games.

"When we would travel, most guys would be in the hotel pool or goofing off," said Ralph Suarez, a teammate on some of the traveling teams that Alex was on. "Alex would be in his room by eight watching ESPN."

Alex didn't watch the games as a casual fan, however; he watched the action the way a young Leonardo da Vinci studied the master painters who had come before him.

"Enjoy your sweat because hard work doesn't guarantee success, but without it, you don't have a chance."

"When I arrived in the big leagues, no one had to tell me that Cal Ripken was a pull hitter, or what Darryl Strawberry did when he had two strikes on him," explained Alex. "My knowledge of these players and my understanding of the game, shortened my learning curve, *big time*."

TWO

TAKING STEPS:
Lost and Found

Although Alex had loved playing baseball ever since he first started having catches with his father during their happy times in the Dominican Republic, during the summer of 1988, when he was 13, he thought about not playing the sport anymore. After hundreds of games in Little League, with the Boys and Girls Club, and travel teams, Alex felt as though baseball had grown stale for him, and he was ready to go in another athletic direction.

"I thought about focusing on basketball, instead," recalled Alex. "Mom called a family meeting, and we talked about my options. She finally convinced me to give baseball one more season."

Alex was such a fine basketball player that, in the fall of 1989, he became the first freshman in two decades to make the varsity at Christopher Columbus High School. He also made the varsity baseball team the following spring, but he didn't get much playing time, and the coach told him that he shouldn't expect to crack the starting line-up until his senior year.

When Hofman spoke to a Miami newspaper about the prospects for the 1991 team, he barely mentioned Alex's name.

Alex's mother hadn't been happy to have him go to a large public school like Columbus, and started to look around at smaller private schools, where she thought that her son might get a better education. Alex's best friend, J.D. Artega, was already enrolled in Westminster Christian, a school with only 300 students, which had a reputation for the academic achievement of its students and also for having a strong athletic program.

J.D. and his father made a big-time recruiting effort to convince Alex and his mom that it was the right place for Alex, and they also told Rich Hofman, Westminster's baseball coach, that Alex was the best young player in Miami.

"People are always telling me about the next Barry Bonds, the second coming of Roger Clemens," said Hofman. "If I believed all the stories, I'd have a team of future Hall of Famers every season."

Although his teams weren't *that* stacked, Hofman had created a powerhouse program, and his 1990 squad had just won the state AA title and finished the season ranked as the tenth best high school team in the nation by *USA Today.*

Fortunately for Alex, he was a good student, a fact that helped earn him a partial scholarship to Westminster, which also made it possible for his mother to more easily afford the thousands of dollars in annual tuition payments.

"I always did my homework, and prepared

myself to succeed in the classroom, just like I did for baseball," said Alex. "I liked doing homework."

During Alex's first semester at West–minster, he suffered a devastating loss, when Juan Artega, who had done so much for him, suffered a heart attack and died, while watching a football game at the school.

"*Keep reading books, stay in school. I encourage kids to read as much as they can, I challenge you to read a book every two weeks, like I try to do.*"

"It was a big blow to me," said Alex. "Everything he gave to A.J., he gave to me. He was the father I didn't have in my life. I still play in his honor."

When Alex reported to baseball practice in the spring of 2001, he discovered that there were 13 players returning from the squad that had won the state title the previous year, and that earning the starting short-stop spot was going to be a major challenge.

"Alex certainly didn't have the look of a superstar," recalled Rich Hofman. "He was a tall, thin, not very strong kid. But you could see by the way that he moved that he was an athlete. That helped him defensively, but he wasn't anywhere close to being a finished product as a hitter."

When the Warriors opened their schedule, Alex was merely one of three shortstops Hofman rotated through the starting lineup as though they were pawns on a chessboard. Although Alex eventually earned the full-time starting nod, it was because of his defensive skills, rather than because of anything he did with his bat.

"He swung at a lot of pitches that weren't even in the same zip code as home plate," recalled Hofman. "He worked hard, but he didn't have any discipline as a hitter."

Although Alex didn't come close to hitting .300 in the spring of 1991, he did rip a 375-foot two-run home run in the district finals, which was all the support that his buddy, J.D., needed in the 10-0 win. Although the 26-6 Warriors altered later on in the state tournament, Alex's disappointment at the loss and at his own problems at the plate, was moderated by the realization that he had made some progress and that he had two more years of baseball to look forward to.

"Mientkiewicz was a tight end, slow but very dependable, great hands. He always thought he was open; no matter how covered he was, he'd come back to the huddle and tell me he was open."

Alex spent the summer working out and building up his body, and by the time he returned to Westminster, he had grown a couple of inches, to 6-2, had added 25 pounds of muscle to his frame, and weighed in at a solid 180 pounds. He put all that muscle to good use on the gridiron in the fall of 1991, when he quarterbacked the Warriors to a 9-1 record, while earning recognition as one of the top prep school quarterbacks in Florida.

One of Alex's top targets was his tight end, Doug Mientkiewicz, who set a school record with 12 touchdown receptions. "Alex had an amazing arm, and he was so quick," said Mientkiewicz, who went on to become a major league first baseman for the Minnesota Twins and the Boston Red Sox. "He probably could have played in the NFL, if he had stuck with football."

After the football season was over, Alex turned in his shoulder pads and laced up his sneakers for the Warriors basketball team. Alex was Westminster's point guard, and was equally adept at running the team, and scorching the nets, as he did one night for 43 points.

"He definitely could have been a big-time college quarterback or point guard," declared James Colzie II, now the cornerbacks coach of Florida State, who beat out Alex for the Dade County Athlete of the Year award for the 1992-93 school year. "He's a phenomenal athlete."

Alex's added muscle also made a big difference in the spring semester, when he hit for a .477 average and swiped 42 bases. His breakout season caught the attention of major league scouts and college recruiters, and also earned him a spot on the 1992 All-America team.

Alex's improvement wasn't solely a matter of added strength, however; it was also a product of all the time he spent at practice, some of it at the home of Mientkiewicz, the team's catcher, who had a batting cage in his backyard.

In high school, some of Alex's friends nicknamed him "Big Dog" and "Big Al." Sometimes they called him "Cheech," after the actor Cheech Marin, of Cheech and Chong fame.

"Alex was always at my house," recalled Mientkiewicz. "Our whole group was pretty close-knit. My house was the flophouse. Even if I didn't go out with those guys one night, they'd be there when I got home."

All that practice paid big dividends for that talented Warriors team, which produced a 32-2 record, won the state title and was named the top prep school team in the country by *Baseball America*.

"Those were great times," said Alex, who also shined in the classroom and earned his way on to Westminster's honor roll. "We were all 15, 16 years old, and we were playing sports all year-round. We went from football to basketball to baseball. That's all a kid wants to do."

That was, actually, Alex's final year of being a three-sport star, however, because after an injury early in the 1992 football season, he decided to skip the rest of the schedule and devote all his athletic energy to baseball, the sport he had almost given up just a few years earlier.

Alex's senior season was pressure-packed from beginning to end. College recruiters were practically camping out on his front lawn, and major league scouts were evaluating his every move in preparation for the amateur draft that would take place on June 3. Alex knew that if he did well, he could make a great deal of money for himself and his family, or have his pick of scholarship offers from a long list of colleges.

"I was just a kid, and scouts were talking

about what I would be doing in two or three years," said Alex. "That's an awful lot of pressure to be under. Especially at that time, when I was so young, and still learning about myself and life."

Alex also benefited from a tip he was given by one of the major league scouts, Larry Corrigan, who is the assistant to the Minnesota Twins' general manager.

"The scouts must be here because they see something they like," explained Alex's mom. "Don't change anything, just be yourself."

"Corrigan was one of the most instrumental people in my career," recalled Alex. "When I was 17 years old in high school, he pulled me aside and told me to stop being a prima donna, and that he would be watching me from that day on. I took the game a lot more seriously and was a lot more focused on the details after that."

Alex was so attentive that he pasted opposing pitching for a .505 average, hammered 9 homers, drove in 36 runs, and swiped

35 bases in 33 games, without being caught even once.

"You can't imagine the pressure he had to go through," said Hofman. "We had big crowds everywhere we played, and they all came to watch Alex. I've never seen a high school player command so much attention.

"I've seen a lot of players who couldn't handle the pressure. Alex thrived on it. It made him work harder."

Although Alex had fashioned a fabulous baseball career at Westminster, and won numerous awards and honors, his final game with the Warriors turned into a painful memory.

Ironically, it had seemed as though Alex was going to be the hero who would lead the Warriors a step closer to a second straight state title, after he blasted a two-run homer that gave them a 7th inning lead in the regional finals, against a team from Palm Beach. But two innings later, Alex turned into the game's goat, when his third error of the day allowed the winning run to cross the plate, ending the Warriors' season and Alex's high school career.

"It's never over," said Hall of Famer and former Yankee catcher, Yogi Berra, "until it's over."

"It was probably the most crushed I've ever been on a baseball field," declared Alex. "That was my last memory before going off to major-league baseball. It was one of those situations that humbled me so much that I felt that, 'Hey, even when you think you are the very best in the country, the No. 1 pick, you can still make the biggest goofball mistake to lose the most important game of the season.'"

THREE

NO. 1:
A Singular Summer

Although Alex's final high school game had ended in disappointment and failure, it didn't dim the luster of his spectacular senior season. During his three years with the Warriors, Alex had gone from being a weak and undisciplined hitter, to becoming a power-hitting shortstop who could drive the ball 400 feet and hit for an astonishingly high average.

Because of his baseball ability, he had had the opportunity to meet high school players from different parts of the world when he competed as a member of the U.S. team in the World Junior Championships in Monterrey, Mexico. And, while Alex led all players with six home runs and tacked on 16 RBI in 13 games, it was the excitement of playing against teams from all over the world that made a lasting impression upon him.

"I don't recall the scores of any of the games," said Alex. "But I do remember how interesting it was to meet players from different cultures."

Alex had also had one of the top thrills of his young life when Cal Ripken, Jr. showed up at one of his games, and then spent some time talking to him.

"Our styles are pretty much alike," Ripken had told reporters afterwards. "Alex has a real good chance to become the best shortstop ever."

"I couldn't wait to run home and tell my family that Cal Ripken knew my name."

Although Ripken's remarks were about some indefinite time in the future, Alex had already established himself as the best high school player in the country. He had been selected as the USA Junior Baseball Player of the Year and the Gatorade National High School Baseball Player of the Year. He had also been the only high school player chosen as a finalist for the Golden Spikes award, which is annually given to the top amateur player in the country. The award almost always goes to a college player, as it did that year, when Darren Dreifort, of Wichita State, was named the winner.

The Seattle Mariners, who held the top pick in the major league amateur–draft in 1993, were also torn between the high school shortstop and the college pitcher. In order to help them make up their minds, the Mariners brought Alex to Seattle for a workout with the team. Alex put on a dazzling hitting and fielding show in the Kingdome, but he impressed the Mariners with his maturity, as much as he did with his superior skills.

"You don't see many guys when they're 17 years old who can walk on to a big league ball field and look like they should stay right there," recalled sportscaster Dave Valle, who was a Seattle catcher at the time. "He looked like he was born to be there. He was a big leaguer, and there were no two ways about it.

And after he made it, he worked even harder. As a player, as a competitor and as an opponent, one of the things people respect about him most is that he shows up to play every day."

"He has all the tools," raved Seattle's former scouting director, Roger Jongewaard. "He can run, hit for average, hit for power, field and throw."

On June 3rd, the Mariners made their selection official by taking Alex with the first pick, while the Los Angeles Dodgers, choosing second, tapped Dreifort.

"He's the best prospect I've ever seen," raved the scouting director of an American League team. "He might be the best player ever in the draft. He's as talented as Ken Griffey, Jr., but he plays with more intensity. The Mariners loved Dreifort, but they couldn't pass on this kid."

Alex received the exciting news while attending a draft-day party with his family and friends at J.D. Arteaga's home. Alex was thrilled to be considered the best amateur player in the nation, but he wasn't happy about being chosen by the Mariners.

Seattle looked like a sad sack franchise at the time, with only one winning season in its 16-year existence. Alex also didn't like the fact that Seattle was further away from home than any other major league city, or that it was an American League team. Alex would have preferred to be selected by a National League team, because then he would at least have the opportunity to play some games in front of his family and friends when the team came to Miami to play against the Marlins.

Later that day, Alex received another phone call, one that he associated more with his past than his future. When he put the receiver to his ear, Alex was shocked to hear the voice of his father, a voice that he hadn't heard since he was nine years old.

"I didn't know what to think," recalled Alex. "It was awkward for both of us, and after a few minutes, he was gone again."

Alex hired sports agent Scott Boras to negotiate his contract with the Mariners, which turned into a long drawn out marathon. While those discussions were going on, Alex became the first high school player ever to be invited to try out for the USA National Team. But that turned into a sour experience, because Alex wouldn't agree to allow Topps, the team sponsor, to create a player card, because they weren't willing to pay him for the use of his picture. When Alex stood his ground, he was cut from the team, and experienced his first taste of the business side of sports.

"My father offered me congratulations, and then we just kind of stumbled through a couple of minutes of small talk. I was too stunned to think."

"If I had signed with them," explained Alex, "it would have cost me at least $500,000 in lost income from another card company."

Later in the summer, as Boras continued to negotiate with Seattle, Alex played for the U.S. Junior National Team against teams of other 17- and 18-year-olds from different countries at the U.S. Sports Festival in San Antonio, Texas. Alex got off to a fast start, smacking four hits in his first two games, but then he was struck just below his right eye by a wildly thrown warm-up toss, which knocked him out and broke his cheekbone.

"If the ball had struck an inch higher, I could have been killed," recalled Alex, who was experiencing the most momentous summer of his young life. "An inch to the side, and I might have lost an eye."

While Alex was recuperating from the accident and waiting for the contract negotiations to finalize, he developed a friendship with Derek Jeter, the young shortstop who had been the New York Yankees top draft pick in the 1992 draft. Jeter was able to provide some insight into how to cope with the lofty expectations that are placed upon a high draft choice, and was also able to give Alex a clue about what life as a minor-leaguer was all about.

But, as the negotiations for a contract

dragged into late August, it seemed as though Alex might be headed to the University of Miami. According to major league rules, if Seattle didn't sign Alex before he attended his first day of classes, they would lose the rights to him, and Alex would become eligible to be selected by another team in the 1994 draft. Finally, on August 30th, the day before Alex was to start his college classes, Boras and the Mariners agreed on a three-year contract that would pay Alex 1.3 million dollars, plus a $1 million signing bonus. At the press conference to announce the deal, Alex was asked what his goal was. His answer was very direct and simple.

"Derek and I hit it off right away. He was a big help, and made it easier for me to adjust to my new situation."

"I want to be in the big leagues as soon as possible."

FOUR

MOVING UP:
Almost Home

Shortly after the contract had been signed, the Mariners brought Alex to Seattle, where he was able to hang out with their superstar center fielder, Ken Griffey, Jr. Griffey, who had been the team's top pick in the 1987 draft, took Alex to dinner and filled him in on what it was like to live and play in Seattle. After dinner, they went back to Griffey's house, where Junior teased Alex about the long bus rides he could expect in the minors, and then they ended their night playing video games.

Almost as soon as the first check from Seattle had cleared the bank, Alex paid off the mortgage on his mother's house, bought her a new car, and gave her all the money she needed to retire.

"My mom is the whole world to me," said Alex. "She deserves everything I can give her, because she's done so much for me."

One of the first things that Alex did after he signed his first contract was to start a scholarship fund at Westminster, so that others could have the opportunity that he had been given.

Alex also bought himself a Jeep, and arranged for Boras to send him a modest monthly allowance. But the remainder of the money was put to work in various investments, which were intended to help secure Alex's financial future, independent of any income that he might make from baseball.

Alex started his professional career a few weeks later, when he took part in the Arizona Instructional League program, where he had the opportunity to work out with other major-league hopefuls. After only a few games, Alex had impressed his team's manager, John McNamara, who'd been a big league manager for three different franchises.

"This kid is the real deal," said McNamara. "He's got real soft hands, terrific range and an A+ arm. He'll have to learn how to hit major league pitching, but he'll adjust. He has as much talent as any teenager that I've ever seen."

After Alex had finished his training in Arizona, he went home to Kendall to prepare himself for the 1994 season. During that time in Florida, Alex worked out almost every day, fielding grounders, hitting against anyone he could find to pitch to him, and lifting weights.

"If I wasn't going to make it, it wasn't going to be because I didn't try my hardest," said Alex. "I knew that nobody was going to be impressed with what I had done in high school. I realized that I was, in a sense, starting out all over again."

Alex experienced his first taste of big-league life early in 1994, when he'd spent a small piece of spring training with the Mariners. But that short stay was enough to show Lou Piniella, who was the Seattle manager, that Alex had the courage that it takes to be successful in the big leagues.

"You get vibes from young players," explained Piniella. "The kid who's scared sits at the end of the bench. When I was ready to make my substitutions, Alex always became very visible. He would grab his glove or his bat, depending upon the situation. In his own way, he was telling me that he was ready."

"I'm not impulsive at all–except about buying clothes. That's my biggest weakness."

But, after a short stay in their camp, he was sent, according to plan, to the Appleton (Wisconsin) Foxes, the franchise's Class A team in the Midwest League. The strategy that had been mapped out by the Mariners staff called for Alex to play half a season with the Foxes, and then, if he played as well as they had hoped he would, for him to move up to their Class AA team in Jacksonville (Florida), in the Southern League.

Alex quickly removed any doubts about

his ability to play at the Class A level. In his first two games, he made a deep impression on one of the opposing players, Joe McEwing, who would go on to play for the St. Louis Cardinals and New York Mets. McEwing watched as Alex, in his first game with Appleton, went deep into the hole between short and third to backhand a hard grounder that had been ticketed for a single to left. Then, he saw Alex pivot around and, in one motion, make a long throw to first to nail the startled runner. McEwing also noticed that Alex looked terrible at the plate in that game, as he watched him strike out twice, while taking feeble swings at curve balls.

"The next night, though, he hit a home run over the left field fence, and lashed a double off the right-center field fence, on the same breaking balls he had looked silly on the night before," recalled McEwing. "You could tell even then that he was pretty special."

Alex, however, did have some darker moments. For one thing, this was his first extended time away from home and, for a few weeks, his batting average hovered around the .280 mark. Although that's a perfectly respectable average for almost any player, especially for one who's in the infancy of his career, it seemed like failure to someone who had become used to banging around pitchers the way Alex had in high school. Alex became so discouraged that he called his mother and told her that he wanted to come home.

"Why do people sing 'Take Me Out to the Ballgame' when they're already there?"

"I don't want you home with *that* defeatist attitude," his mother scolded. "You go out and play hard, and everything will be fine."

Alex responded to that pep talk by going on a 16-game hitting rampage, during which he rapped 11 home runs, knocked in 31 runs, and hit for a .406 average.

"You can spend a lifetime as a manager and never see a player of his caliber," said

Carlos Lezcano, Alex's Appleton manager. "It wasn't only what he did with the stick, he fielded his position with the grace of a ballet dancer, and he ran the bases like a deer."

In addition to his on-field abilities, Alex also demonstrated a likeable personality and a down-to-earth character, which impressed his teammates.

"I don't know anyone who doesn't like Alex," said Raul Ibanez, one of Alex's teammates at Appleton. "You knew he was a No. 1 pick and got a nice contract, and would go to the majors quick. But he was good with everyone, just one of the guys on the club."

After playing in only 65 games with Appleton, Alex was promoted to Jacksonville, a journey that usually takes even fast-rising players at least a year to make. The majority of players at the Double A level have already had at least two seasons in the minors under their belt, and most of them are in their early 20's. Alex, however, was unfazed by his quick promotion, and announced his arrival to the Southern League by hammering a home run in his first at-bat.

On July 7th, after only 17 games with Jacksonville, during which time he hit .288, Alex was told to pack his bags and fly to Boston, where Seattle was scheduled to play a three-day weekend series against the Red Sox. The following day, only 13 months after he had graduated from high school, Alex made his major-league debut in fabled Fenway Park, and became the youngest player to play in the big leagues since Jose Rijo joined the New York Yankees in 1984, 37 days shy of his 19th birthday.

"We have a problem here," said Piniella. "If we didn't have a problem, Alex wouldn't be here yet."

"If it doesn't work out, I'm the one who's going to be criticized," said Lou Piniella. "I lobbied the front office to bring him up."

Piniella knew that he might be rushing Alex into a situation that his 18-year-old shortstop wasn't ready to handle, especially when it came to hitting big league pitching after only a short stint in the minors. But the manager had been unhappy with the glove work of his middle infielders, and he hoped that Alex could help shore up Seattle's leaky defense.

"Let's face it, if we were in the middle of a pennant race, we would have left him at Jacksonville," acknowledged Piniella. "But we're not even playing .500 ball, and we figured he'd be ready next year, anyway. So, I'm just pushing the button a little faster than I thought I would."

Although Alex wasn't at all assured that he was capable of facing major league pitching after so little time at Jacksonville, he tried to reassure Piniella by telling his skipper, "Don't worry, I know I'm ready."

Even after Alex drew the collar in his first game, going 0-for-3, there wasn't a happier person in Beantown.

"Last year I would have paid anything to watch a major league game," said Alex, only the third 18-year-old shortstop since 1900 to play in the majors. "This year I'm playing in one."

Alex did collect a pair of hits in his second game, and also swiped a base. Two days later, with the Mariners home, and facing the Yankees, Alex showed Piniella the type of defense that he had been looking for, when he flagged down a bouncer up the middle with a diving stab of his outstretched glove. As he tumbled to the ground, Alex switched the ball to his right hand and came up throwing, all in one sweet, acrobatic motion. The throw thumped into the first baseman's glove a moment before the speedy Bernie Williams touched the bag, and drew a standing ovation from the Seattle fans.

"I gave it my best shot, but at 18 years old, I wasn't ready to hit against major league pitchers."

But the holes in Alex's swing were quickly exposed by major-league pitchers, and after only 17 games, Alex and his .204 average were sent packing to the Mariners Class AAA team in Calgary, Alberta, Canada.

In his 32-game stint in the Pacific Coast League, Alex showed that he could hit at the top level of the minor leagues by pasting Pacific Coast League pitching for six homers, 21 RBI and a .311 average.

"It could have been easy to get down on myself, but I wasn't going to let a disappointment derail me."

Although Alex hadn't been ready to hold his own against major league pitching, his remarkably rapid rise through the Mariners minor league system had convinced the team that they had a rising star on their horizon.

FIVE

SEATTLE TO TACOMA AND BACK:
The Yo-Yo Blues

Although Alex had made amazing strides in his first season in professional baseball, he wasn't content to sit around in the off-season and read his press clippings. He, instead, decided to play Winter League Baseball in the Dominican Republic, where he hoped to improve his skills and get a head start on the 1995 season.

Alex liked being back in the Dominican, a place that evoked fond memories of his childhood, and where he still had lots of family to visit with. But, on the field, Alex seemed overmatched, and the season quickly turned into a horror show.

"It was the toughest experience of my life,"

said Alex, who hit for a .179 average during his three months of utter futility. "I kept thinking I was going to turn things around, but I never did. I just got my tail kicked, and learned how hard this game can be. It was brutal, but I recommend it to every young player."

As if he wasn't frustrated and anxious enough about his horrendous hitting, Alex received a startling shock to his system when his father showed up one afternoon at the stadium.

"I was taking batting practice," recalled Alex, who hadn't seen Victor in more than ten years. "When he told me who he was, I almost broke down, right on the field. I told him that I would go to lunch with him the next day."

But Alex was still too filled with bitterness towards his father to want to spend time with him, so he cancelled the plans.

"I couldn't go and see him just like that," said Alex. "I wasn't ready to let go of all my anger and hurt."

Despite the hard knocks that Alex had taken

during the 1994 season and in the Dominican Winter League, he was hopeful that a strong performance in spring training would allow him to begin the 1995 season as Seattle's starting shortstop. But that hope eventually turned into despair, as Alex spent most of the season bouncing between Seattle and their Triple-A team in Tacoma, Washington.

Alex dominated the Pacific Coast League during his stays with the Rainiers, hitting at a .354 clip, while hacking 15 homers and piling up 45 RBI in 54 games. Although Alex didn't do nearly as well in the 48 games he played with the Mariners, he did try to learn as much as he could from the team's top players.

"Sometimes, the best lessons that we get in life come with hard edges."

"He wanted to learn from everyone around him," said David Valle, a catcher on the team. "He asked me about what it was like when I was drafted. He was always taking as much from Edgar Martinez and Junior Griffey as he could. With as much talent as he had, he never acted in a way that said, 'I don't need anybody's help.'"

Alex received a lesson-by-example in what it takes to excel as a big leaguer from Martinez, the Mariners designated hitter. Alex had left the Kingdome after an early afternoon practice on a non-playing date, but went back four hours later to retrieve the cell phone that he had left behind. When he walked into the otherwise deserted clubhouse, he heard the thump of a bat against a ball, and found Martinez still in the underground batting cage, working on the stroke that would earn him the 1995 A.L. batting championship, his second title in four years. When Alex asked his teammate why he was still there, Martinez had a simple answer.

"Hitting is my job," said Martinez, who retired after the 2004 season with a .312 career batting average. "And I have to put in the practice time to do it as well as I want to."

Alex did a mental double-take at the realization that an established big-league batting champion was taking all those extra hours of batting practice, while he had been relaxing all afternoon.

"Seeing Edgar made me realize that there were levels to the game, and that I needed to put in even more work than I was doing, if I wanted to keep moving upward."

The lessons, however, weren't always pain-less. After one particularly inept strikeout, Piniella had looked as though smoke might blow out of his nostrils.

"I want to be known as a good major-leaguer, and good major-leaguers work to become good."

"You've got to give me better swings than *that*," growled the manager, as Alex sat in the dugout, and put on his sunglasses to hide the tears he felt welling up. Piniella, however, sensed that Alex needed a pat more than a scold, so he walked over to his struggling shortstop and kissed him on the forehead.

"In that one moment, he showed me toughness and love," recalled Alex. "It meant so much to me that he cared enough to do that."

The constant bouncing back and forth between Tacoma and Seattle, however, began to eat away at Alex's usually positive attitude. And while the trip between Seattle and the Rainiers home field took only thirty minutes, it seemed like an eternity to Alex every time he was sent back down.

"Each demotion chipped away at my confidence," recalled Alex. "The last time, in mid-August, I sat at my Seattle locker with my head down, in tears. I felt drained, defeated."

Alex was so discouraged that he briefly thought about quitting baseball, and enrolling at the University of Miami.

"I have *nothing* left to prove at triple-A," he told his mother. "I want to play in the majors. Maybe it would have been better if I had gone to college. Hopefully, next year I'll have *one* address."

Alex was called back to Seattle for the fourth and final time on August 31st, which gave him a ringside seat for Seattle's season-ending surge. Griffey had been sidelined with an injury for most of the season, and despite strong hitting by Martinez, and a Cy Young Award-winning season from pitcher Randy Johnson, the Mariners were still 11.5 games out of first place when Griffey returned to the lineup on August 24th.

"It was breakfast, lunch, dinner and good night," said Alex, as he recalled his hapless strikeout by former Oakland A's ace, Dennis Eckersley. *"I didn't have a clue, or a prayer."*

Junior had immediately made his presence known by cracking a game-winning home run in his first game back, a spark that lit the fuse on a classic stretch run that enabled the Mariners to overtake the Texas Rangers and end the season tied for first place in the American

League Western Division with the Angels.

The Mariners, who had taken to wearing T-shirts imprinted with the motto, "Refuse to Lose," beat up the Angels 9-1 in a one-game playoff, and brought the first division title home to Seattle. Next up were the Yankees, who swept the first two games of the Division Series in New York. The teams then moved to the Kingdome, where the Mariners, with their backs to the wall, took the next pair of games, to knot the best-of-five series at two games each.

The decisive game turned into a classic post-season struggle between two teams who were each fighting to play another day. Junior had given the hometown fans reason to cheer when he hit a seventh inning home run that put the Mariners in the lead, 4-3. The Yankees, though, silenced the Kingdom with a run in the ninth, and then sent a shiver through the Seattle fans when they pushed across another run two innings later.

The Mariners, however, had lived up to the words on their T-shirts, as Martinez delivered a two-run double in the bottom of the inning, which scored second baseman Joey Cora and Junior, who had raced home from first base. Alex, who had entered the game in the eighth inning, was in the on-deck circle, waiting for his chance to hit. But as he watched Griffey streaking toward the plate, he started pumping his palms up and down, signaling Junior to *slide, slide, slide.*

"It's kind of ironic, isn't it? At first I didn't want to play in Seattle," said Alex, in the joyous clubhouse immediately after the game. "Now I can't imagine playing anywhere else. This is the perfect place for me."

Although the Mariners dropped the American League Championship to

Edgar Martinez received the 2004 Roberto Clemente Award, which is given annually to the player who combines outstanding baseball skill with a devotion to community service.

Cleveland, that loss couldn't erase the excitement that Alex had felt as the team made its charge. And he was also buoyed by the sense that, despite all the hard times and disappointments, his time was about to come.

"Being a part of that 1995 team was an awesome experience. I knew I wasn't ready to be a regular, but I still loved being involved in the excitement."

"Alex is going to start next year," predicted Luis Sojo, the incumbent Seattle shortstop. "He has so much talent, it's unbelievable. He's like the second coming of Junior."

SIX

SIZZLING IN SEATTLE:
One of a Kind

Although Alex came to spring training in 1996 as the team's top shortstop candidate, he still had to prove that he could hit for a higher average than the anemic .232 he had managed the previous season. Piniella had counted on Alex to pick up the pace, based upon his two years of experience, but even the manager wasn't prepared for the sudden makeover in which Alex went from being a wild-swinging novice to a disciplined and selective hitter.

"It came almost overnight," said Piniella. "It wasn't there at all one week, and, suddenly, the next week there it was. And then, he just kept getting better and better."

Although Alex's transformation as a hitter

seemed almost magical, the seeds of his startling improvement had been planted before he ever arrived at training camp. The results that seemed so sudden to Piniella were, actually, the fruits of Alex's willingness to work hard and to listen and learn from the people who could help him fulfill the potential that everyone knew was waiting to bust out.

Alex had worked hard between seasons, and he had also spent countless hours watching tapes of Edgar Martinez, who had hit for a .356 average in 1995.

"The tapes were three hours long, all his hits from the previous two seasons," explained Alex. "I watched them about three times a week. If you have a great hitter to learn from, it makes a lot of sense to study how they get it done."

When Alex arrived at spring training and had trouble getting untracked, he went to the Mariners hitting coach, Lee Elia, and asked for more help.

"His swing was too long," recalled Elia.

"He didn't have good bat control. We worked four, five days shortening his swing, getting him to understand that he had enough bat speed to drive the ball without taking a real long swing.

"In the first game he played after those sessions, he stroked a couple of hits," contin-ued Elia. "That made him feel comfortable, and he went into the season in a good frame of mind."

"I haven't seen too many guys who can get their bats through the hitting zone any faster than Alex," said Lee Elia. "With his ability, there's no telling what he can accomplish."

All the work that Alex had done started paying dividends almost immediately. Early in May, after Piniella saw that Alex was for real, he put him in the second slot in the batting order, directly in front of Griffey, Martinez and Buhner.

Hitting in front of that run-producing trio made it even easier for Alex to be selective, since pitchers didn't want to take a chance on putting him on base in front of the dangerous hitters that followed him.

Alex responded to Piniella's show of faith by going on a two-month tear in which he hit .361, which landed him a berth on the American League All-Star team, behind starter Cal Ripken.

"He's a big, physical shortstop like Ripken, but he's a better athlete," said veteran general manager John Hart, who was comparing Alex to the dominant shortstop of the era. "He probably has more power than Cal, and he might be a better all-around hitter."

"I doubt that I had that much talent when I was starting out," agreed Ripken. "He has talent that flows with every action he takes."

Three weeks after he had become the youngest shortstop ever to play in an All-Star Game, Alex's 21st birthday present from the Mariners was a four-year, $10.5 million contract extension. A few hours later, Alex began earning the money by hitting his 27th home run of the season. The contract extension was a major vote of confidence for Alex, who had thought that he might be traded for a front-line pitcher, a commodity that was in short supply for the pitching-starved Mariners.

"It was a great day, an emotional day," said Alex, who announced that he had founded *Grand Slam for Kids*, which encourages children to work harder on reading, physical fitness, math and good citizenship. "It was really special to have my family and Rich Hofman, my high school coach here. It shows how far you can go with sacrifice, commitment and hard work."

"He has a sense of history for the game that sets him apart from lots of today's players," said Piniella. "He's the real McCoy."

Alex, who had become universally known as A-Rod, continued to stroke the ball through the dog days of August, and hit in a career-high 20 straight games between August 16th and September 4th.

"He learned in a couple of years what it took me ten years to learn," declared Edgar Martinez. "He goes with the pitch, and uses the whole field, foul pole to foul pole."

Alex had learned so well that he wound up leading the American League in hitting, with a .358 average, the highest average by a right-handed hitter since Yankee Hall of Famer Joe DiMaggio batted .381 in 1939. Alex, who also stroked 36 home runs and knocked in 123 runs, produced the best season ever by a 21-year-old, and became the third-youngest player to win a batting title, after Hall of Famers Al Kaline and Ty Cobb.

"It's obvious to everyone that he's a special player," said Ripken. "And the thing that impresses me the most is his maturity. He plays the game like he's been in the league four or five years."

Alex's outrageous hitting earned him his first Silver Slugger Award, as the League's best-hitting shortstop, and his slick fielding made him the runner-up for the Gold Glove Award, behind Cleveland's Omar Vizquel.

"I'd rather have a Gold Glove than a Silver Slugger Award," said Alex, who made only 15 errors, five less than Vizquel. "Defense is so much more of a team game than hitting."

Alex also came in second in the voting for the League's Most Valuable Player Award, as the Baseball Writers Association of America gave the nod, by only three votes, to Juan Gonzalez, who had also had an outstanding year for the Texas Rangers. The decisive factor for some of the voters was that Gonzalez had helped lead the Rangers to their first American League West Division championship, while the Mariners, despite Alex's heroics, had finished second. He was, however, named *The Sporting News* Player of the Year,

"He's a smart kid, and he works hard," said Griffey. *"He just has to listen and learn the game. Everyone knows he's going to be a special player."*

an award that is voted upon by major league players.

Alex, who finished among the league leaders in 11 offensive categories, had compiled the most productive season by any shortstop in the history of baseball. But, as soon as the season ended, he was already looking forward to a brighter future.

"I love the challenge of the game," said Alex, who remembered the struggles he'd endured in the previous two years. "I love the work. My goal right now is to have a season next year that will make people forget about this one. I'm pumped. I'm hungry."

"The way he's going, someday he might bat .400 and hit 60 home runs," said veteran baseball executive Dan Duquette. *"He's the best young talent I've seen for years."*

SEVEN

40—40:
Moving On

Although he was just as driven to succeed as he had ever been, a June collision with Toronto Blue Jays pitcher Roger Clemens sidelined Alex for two weeks, and the bruised ribs that he suffered dogged him throughout the remainder of the 1997 season.

"I came back too soon," said Alex, who still managed to become the first A.L. shortstop since 1983, other than Ripken, to start an All-Star Game. "I wasn't able to throw the way I should, or swing the bat anywhere near what I was capable of. I was playing hurt, but I wanted to be out there."

The inability to play at a hundred percent sent Alex's offensive numbers into a nosedive, and he wound up hitting only 23 homers, with 84 RBI and a .300 batting average. Although those numbers would have thrilled almost any other player of Alex's age and experience, they weren't the numbers expected of a rising superstar.

The Mariners, however, had so much firepower and pitching that they were able to overcome Alex's decreased production and still take their second divisional title with 90 wins, the most in franchise history. Griffey led the charge with 57 home runs and 147 RBI, and was named the A.L. MVP. Martinez and Buhner delivered as expected, and second baseman Joey Cora, first baseman Paul Sorrento and catcher Dan Wilson also played important roles, as the team mashed a major league-record 264 home runs. Randy Johnson was, again, the mainstay of the pitching staff, and went 20-4, with a 2.28 earned run average and 291 Ks in only 213 innings.

After all those wins and offensive fireworks during the season, however, the Mariners were blown away by Baltimore in the Divisional Playoff Series, 3-games-to-1, as the Orioles pitchers held the power-hitting Mariners to a total of 11 runs in the four games. All of Seattle's stars faded away during the series, other than Alex, who hit .312 and cracked his first post-season home run. Ripken, though, stood tall for the Orioles, leading all hitters with a .438 average.

Randy Johnson has won 5 Cy Young Awards and struck out 4,161 batters, the third highest total in "major league" history.

"What I do as an individual has always been less important to me than what the team does," said Alex. "I want to help Seattle win a World Series."

The 1998 season will long be remembered as one of the most exciting in baseball history, as Mark McGwire, with 70 four-baggers, and Sammy Sosa, with 66, both eclipsed the all-time single-season home run record, which had stood at 61 since 1961, when Roger Maris had slipped by the record of 60, which had been set by Babe Ruth in 1927.

For the Mariners, 1998 will be remembered as a season of missed opportunities, and the start of an exodus, which would see three of its superstars gone by the end of the decade.

Seattle had started the season with great expectations, based upon their strong showing in 1997, but 1998 turned out to be a season of individual brilliance and collective failure.

The root of the problem for the Mariners was its pitching staff, which had depended on Randy Johnson to be its ace and anchor. Johnson, however, was in the last year of his contract with the Mariners and when he couldn't negotiate the contract terms that he wanted, he simply went into a funk. By the end of July, relations between Johnson and the team had reached a point of no return, so the 6' 10" left-hander, with his 9-10 record and bulging ERA, was traded to the Houston Astros.

The offense, meanwhile, had picked up where it had left off in 1997, with Griffey, who whacked 56 home runs and notched 146 RBI, becoming only the third player to hit 50 dingers and swipe 20 bases in the same season. Alex had also written lines into the record book, by becoming only the third player to hit 40 home runs and steal 40 bases in the same season. Jose Canseco, when he played for the A's, had been the first to accomplish that rare display of power and speed, in 1988, and Barry Bonds had followed suit in 1996.

Barry Bonds set a new single-season record when he hit 73 home runs in 2001. He is currently third on the all-time list with 703.

With the Mariners well out of the division race, the excitement in Seattle was all about Alex's attempt to hit No. 40, which went down to the final week of the season. When he finally connected off of Anaheim's Jack McDowell, it was as if a collective sigh had swept through Seattle.

"There was a lot of pressure to hit that homer, so it was tough," recalled Alex. "When

I ran around the bases, I felt like I was *floating.*"

Three days later, Alex tagged his 41st homer to break the A.L. record for home runs by a shortstop, which had been set by Boston's Rico Petrocelli in 1969.

"Winning is the most important thing to me, so I'm disappointed that we're not going to make it to the post-season," said Alex, who wound up the season with 42 dingers and 46 stolen bases. "But, from an individual standpoint, reaching the 40-40 mark has to rank as the most memorable moment of my baseball career."

Although the Mariners moved out of the Kingdome and into Safeco Field on July 15th, the 1999 season turned into an eerie echo of 1998, as they compiled a dreary 79-83 record, and finished 16 games out of first place. Alex, who had missed an early chunk of the season due to torn cartilage in his left knee, came back strong and nearly replicated the numbers he had posted the year before. Although he played in only 123 games, he still hammered out 42 home runs and knocked in 111 runs.

"Alex has become a great player in a short time," declared Edgar Martinez. "He can run, throw, and field. He can hit for average and for power. And he's also a very mature person, who has handled fame and attention extremely well."

"This is just the beginning," said Seattle hitting coach, Jesse Barfield. *"He's going to shatter a lot of records in his career."*

As it turned out, though, the Mariners didn't suffer their biggest loss until after the season ended, when they traded Griffey, at his request, to the Cincinnati Reds, Junior's hometown team.

During the four seasons that Alex had played full-time with Griffey, the centerfielder had *averaged* 52 home runs and 141 RBI, and won the final four of his 10 consecutive A.L. Gold Gloves.

"He was electric," said Alex. "He'd climb outfield walls as if he was Spiderman, and I had a great seat every night. He's the best player I've ever seen on a baseball field, *period.*"

With Randy Johnson and Junior gone, Alex and Edgar Martinez had become the dual leaders of a newly constructed Mariners team in 2000. Mike Cameron, who had come over in the Griffey trade, took over in centerfield, and general manager Pat Gillick had signed free-agent first baseman John Olerud. Gillick had fortified the pitching staff by signing Aaron Sele, who had been a 19-game winner for Texas in 1999, and had imported Kazuhiro Sasaki from Japan to be the team's bullpen closer.

Gillick had done his job well, and the Mariners looked as though they were a good bet to take the division title until the next-to-last weekend of the season, when they dropped 3-of-4 to the hard charging Oakland A's. Alex, with one hit in 16 at-bats, had looked helpless against the A's, and was snared in a sorry slump with only two games left in a season that was slipping away.

"Let's be honest, he's the heart and soul of this team," said Piniella, who was hoping to catch the A's or, at least, hold off Cleveland, who were challenging for the wild-card spot. "If he doesn't break out, we're not going to win the race to the finish line. We need Alex to get hot."

In 1998, Ken Griffey, Jr. became the youngest player to reach 350 home runs; in 1999, his fellow players selected him as the Player of the Decade.

As if in answer to Piniella's wish, Alex broke out of his slump with four hits against the Angels, including a pair of home runs, which gave him 40 dingers for the third consecutive season. Seattle also won a must-win game the following day, and secured the wild card in the West on the final day of the schedule.

"I feel this was the first year I had to lead, and it was emotionally draining," said Alex, who had made it clear that he was going to become a free agent at the end of the season.

"I know I sucked against the A's, but in the last couple of days, when our backs were against the wall, I feel proud that I somewhat answered the call."

Alex continued to shoulder the load in the postseason, as Seattle swept three games from the Chicago White Sox in the Division Series, before falling to the Yankees in the ALCS, 4-games-to-2.

Although Alex hadn't been able to lift Seattle over the collective superiority of the Yankees, his clutch hitting in the final weekend of the season, and his .371 average in the post-season, had only enhanced his value in the free-agent bazaar that was about to begin.

"He's the type of player you build an organization around," said Jay Buhner. *"Performers like him don't come around very often. He's like Junior. He does everything, and he does it effortlessly."*

EIGHT

THE LONE RANGER: 252 and Skidoo

Alex had finished among the league leaders in virtually every offensive category in the 2000 season, and at 25-years-old, with his prime years still in front of him, he was the most prized free-agent ever to enter the market.

Alex would have preferred to stay in Seattle, if the Mariners showed him that they had a plan to upgrade the team and pay him whatever the going rate turned out to be.

"I can tell you I am seriously considering the Mariners," said Alex, after the season. "But there aren't going to be any hometown discounts. I've done that before. Not this time."

The Mets were Alex's second choice, and he didn't make any secret of the fact that New York was his favorite city, and that he would wel-come the opportunity to play for the team.

"I was a *huge* Mets fan; I watched every game in '86, Kiner's *Korner*, Tim McCarver, the whole thing," said Alex, referring to two of the team's announcers and a post-game televi-sion show. "My favorite player was Keith Hernandez. I *loved* him. I loved *everything* about him."

Mets management also seemed to have a big-time interest in obtaining Alex, an exciting young ballplayer, who could provide a major impact on the field, and help the team com-pete for fans and attention against the Yankees, their Big Apple rivals.

The expectation that Alex would sign with the Mets was raised to a fever pitch when he showed up at Yankee Stadium to watch the Bronx Bombers play against the Mets in the 2000 World Series. Alex insisted that he had come to New York just to cheer on his friend Derek Jeter. But, while Alex told that tale to the media, the story that he told his friends was that he was hoping to sign with the Mets for 10 years, and around $190 million.

It seemed like a perfect match between a player who wanted to play on the biggest stage and a team from the biggest of all markets, which needed a great player to compete on the field, and a marquee name to draw fans and television viewers, as well as to sell merchandise.

"I don't base my goals on numbers. All of my goals are based on my work ethic and my preparation."

The Mets, however, quickly and surprisingly, took themselves out of the hunt, and the Mariners didn't step up to the plate with a suitable plan or enough dollars. Alex was disappointed that he didn't get to sign with either of his top two choices, and was sorry to be leaving Lou Piniella.

"He was the most influential person in my baseball career," said Alex. "I met him when I was 17 and left him at 25, so I started with him as a boy and left as a man. I always hear his voice when I'm playing, because he'd always let you know when you screwed up."

But, Alex's disappointment was soon displaced by the efforts of Texas Rangers owner, Tom Hicks, who signed him to a $252 million, ten-year deal—*more than twice as much money* as any baseball player had ever before been guaranteed.

The numbers were so staggering that there wasn't really any rational frame of reference in which to view them. Although Alex was thrilled about signing his name on the bottom line, he realized the contract was, by any measure, outsized.

"It's almost embarrassing to talk about," said Alex. "I don't know if Michael Jordan, or Bill Gates, or *Alexander the Great*, or *anyone* is worth this type of money, but that's the market we're in today. That's what Mr. Hicks decided to pay me, and now it's time to pay him back and win a couple of championships."

Alex delivered even more than was expected of him during his three-year stay in Texas, but his hitting heroics were never enough to lift the pitching-poor Rangers out of the divisional cellar, let alone lead them to a championship.

Ironically, the 2001 All-Star Game was held at Safeco Field, where Alex was joined by a contingent of *eight* Seattle players, and was greeted with a loud round of boos from the Seattle fans, who felt that Alex had deserted them. But Alex did have a ringside seat when Cal Ripken socked a home run in his last All-Star appearance and was named the game's MVP.

"I've taken a couple of golf lessons from Tiger Woods.
He's a good friend. It's more enjoyable to take a lesson from him than to play against him."

Despite the pressure that the outsized contract had placed on him, Alex went on to lead the league with 52 dingers and 133 runs scored, and finished third in RBI (135) and slugging percentage (.622), while hitting .318.

Meanwhile, no one could have blamed Alex if he had turned an envious eye towards the northwest, where Ichiro Suzuki, who was named the MVP and Rookie of the Year, led Seattle to an American League-record 116 wins.

Alex stepped up his production even further in 2002, as he led the majors in home runs, with 57, and RBI's, with 142, and finished second, behind Yankee second baseman, Alfonso Soriano, in runs scored (123), fourth in slugging percentage (.623), while hitting an even .300. Alex also staked a clear claim to being the game's best all-around player by winning the first of his two consecutive Gold Gloves Awards for fielding excellence.

"He came to the ballpark every day from the first day of spring training until the last day of the season, like he was a utility infielder," said Jerry Narron, who managed the Rangers in 2001 and 2002. "He worked as hard as any player I've ever been around."

Rafael Palmeiro, who slugged 43 four-baggers and drove in 105 runs, and catcher Ivan Rodriguez also did their parts to try to lift the team out of last place. But the rest of the roster was littered with journeymen and young players, like second baseman Michael Young and third baseman Hank Blalock, who weren't ready to deliver prime-time performances.

Although Alex didn't have the joy of playing in the post-season, he did have the best off-season of his life because, on November 2nd, he married Cynthia Scurtis, a high school psychology teacher.

"One of the coolest experiences I've ever had is playing 72 holes of golf with Bill Gates. That was pretty special."

"The day I got married was the most memorable day of my life," said Alex. "The next one will be the day my first child is born. That will be the most special day in my life."

Cynthia has used her training in psychology to help Alex and his father reconcile with one other.

"Any time your father isn't around, there is a void," said Cynthia, who made the initial phone call to Victor. "When I met Alex I felt Alex owed it to himself to find out and make his own judgment as an adult. Every child has a mother and father, it's not about picking."

"As a kid you want everything to be perfect, and you don't understand the nature of divorce," said Alex. "With Cynthia's help, I was able to understand that many relationships don't work out. She gave me the courage to get things going."

But, try as he might, Alex wasn't able to get anything going in Texas, even though he tied for the major league in homers in 2003, while finishing among the league leaders in virtually every major hitting category, and becoming only the second player from a last place team to win a league MVP Award.

The only other player on a last-place team to win an MVP was Andre Dawson, who won it when he played for the Chicago Cubs in 1987.

By the end of the season, Alex had decided that he wanted out of Texas. He wasn't happy with Texas manager Buck Showalter, and piling up huge stats and awards didn't mean very much without the challenge of playing for a team that could contend for a championship.

NINE

COMING HOME:
Pinstriped Dreams

Alex and Tom Hicks had come together with the best of intentions, but after three fruitless, last-place seasons, they both realized that it was time to separate.

"It's a lot easier to play well when you're having fun, and winning is obviously a lot more fun than losing," explained Alex. "Last season was the toughest of my career because of that. I was overcome with a sense of depression. There were days I didn't want to go to the ballpark. That had never happened to me before."

Alex had lived up to his high-paying contract by averaging 52 home runs and 132 RBI, while posting three of the best seasons that any player has ever strung together.

"Alex was our leader," said Tom Hicks, who had come to realize that a lone superstar couldn't transform a franchise. "He was always coming up with ideas how he thought the team could be improved. Alex played his heart out for three years."

The off-season had turned into an emotional roller coaster for Alex, who at first thought that he was headed to the Red Sox, and then despaired that he was stuck with the Rangers for another sorry season. Shortly before the start of spring training, however, lightning struck, and Alex was traded to the Yankees for All-Star second baseman Alfonso Soriano. Alex was so happy to be returning to the city of his birth and to play for a perennial contender, that he agreed to switch from shortstop, a position already manned in New York by team captain Derek Jeter, to third base.

"I grew up with a Cal Ripken Jr. poster over my bed, and I wanted to reach certain goals as a shortstop, but that doesn't matter to me anymore," said Alex. "I'm more interested in the prospect of winning a championship, and I'm looking forward to the new challenge."

Alex's arrival in New York also delighted the large Dominican population in Washington Heights, where he had been born.

"You're talking about the Latin Babe Ruth," declared Miguel Montas, the owner of a neighborhood restaurant, which is often frequented by Dominican players when they come to New York. "The Latin people have a message today to Yankees owner, George Steinbrenner: Thank you for doing this for us."

"I have never seen Alex so happy," said Eddie Rodriguez, still one of Alex's closet friends. "He's in the best shape of his life. When the Yankee deal happened, he was like a little kid he was so excited."

"My work ethic comes from my mother. I just make sure I give it my best effort. Results are not something I really judge myself on, it's the steps and the ladder, the everyday routine."

Putting on the pinstriped uniform and playing in Yankee Stadium, the most hallowed field in baseball, presents unique challenges, however. There's the vaunted history, which caused Alex to switch the number on his jersey from '3' to '13', since the lower number had been worn by the great Babe Ruth, and was one of the many numbers that the team had retired. The entire organization, from the owner to the players, judged the success of each season by only one criterion: Winning the World Series.

"You're not paid to win 100 games here," explained team executive and Hall of Famer Reggie Jackson, who had earned the nickname "Mr. October," when he played for the Yankees. "You're not paid to take us from 102 wins to 109. You're paid to win the last 11."

"I've seen this guy play for a long time and when you look at him, you basically see the best player in baseball and maybe the best player of all time," said former teammate and Yankee coach Luis Sojo.

Alex started the 2004 season horridly, flailing at pitches out of the strike zone and compiling a .160 average through his first 50 at-bats.

"That was the first time in my career I felt

totally helpless, totally out of control," he acknowledged. "I wasn't ready for that, and I didn't like that feeling at all."

For the first time in four years, Alex was playing for a contending team, and he found that he had to stop putting too much pressure on himself.

"He could play at any position," said Don Zimmer, who has been involved with baseball for more than half a century. "Third, short, second, first or all three outfield positions—and he'd be an All-Star at every one of them."

"When he goes up to the plate, he expects magic to happen all the time," said Yankees manager Joe Torre. "That's very tough to live up to."

"A lot of times I feel like a rookie here," said Alex. "My biggest adjustment has been to control my emotions and realize that while every game's important, we're not at the seventh game of the World Series, yet."

Alex eventually managed to dig himself out of the hole he had dug earlier in the season, and wound up hitting .286, with 35 homers and 108 RBI, but he hit only .248 with runners in scoring position, and his productivity didn't come close to matching what he had accomplished in the previous seven seasons.

"Nothing has been easy this year," acknowledged Alex, before the Yankees began the Division Series against the Minnesota Twins. "But I feel like my best baseball is ahead of me."

Alex then proceeded to play his best ball of the season, hitting .421 and leading the Yanks to a 3-games-to-1 win over the Twins. Alex iced the series for the Yanks in the 11th inning of Game 4, when he stroked a double off Kyle Lohse, stole third, then scored the winning run when the unhinged Lohse threw a wild pitch.

"When you think you've seen everything he can do, he continues to amaze you," said Yankees right fielder Gary Sheffield. "He's the best player in the game, and he showed that tonight."

Alex continued to pound the baseball against Boston in the ALCS, as the Yankees swept the first three games of the series. But, just when it counted most, Alex was a feeble

2-for-17, as the Red Sox swept the final four games, and became the first major league team to overcome a 3-0 deficit in the post-season.

"Nothing came easy this year," said Alex.

"I just hope that I can reach my ultimate potential, whatever that is."

"But we'll be back next year, and the year after that. I know I'll have the chance to play for a championship every season, and that's all I can ask for."

"As good as he is, he still has growth potential," noted Reggie Jackson. "He's been here one year and the expectations and all that's gone on, that's part of the growth process."

"A-Rod's on a pace with Ruth, Henry Aaron and Willie Mays," added Jackson, comparing Alex to three legends of the game. "He hasn't reached it yet, but he deserves the recognition for being where he is. He's here because one day his record will compare to the legacy of Ruth, Lou Gehrig and all the great Yankee players of the past."

ALEX RODRIGUEZ CAREER STATS

— Regular Season Hitting Stats —

SEASON	TEAM	G	AB	R	H	2B	3B	HR	RBI	TB	BB	SO	SB	CSO	BP	SLG	AVG
1994	Seattle Mariners	17	54	4	11	0	0	0	2	11	3	20	3	0	.241	.204	.204
1995	Seattle Mariners	48	142	15	33	6	2	5	19	58	6	42	4	2	.264	.408	.232
1996	Seattle Mariners	146	601	141	215	54	1	36	123	379	59	104	15	4	.414	.631	.358
1997	Seattle Mariners	141	587	100	176	40	3	23	84	291	41	99	2	6	.350	.496	.300
1998	Seattle Mariners	161	686	123	213	35	5	42	124	384	45	121	46	13	.360	.560	.310
1999	Seattle Mariners	129	502	110	143	25	0	42	111	294	56	109	21	7	.357	.586	.285
2000	Seattle Mariners	148	554	134	175	34	2	41	132	336	100	121	15	4	.420	.606	.316
2001	Texas Rangers	162	632	133	201	34	1	52	135	393	75	131	18	3	.399	.622	.318
2002	Texas Rangers	162	624	125	187	27	2	57	142	389	87	122	9	4	.392	.623	.300
2003	Texas Rangers	161	607	124	181	30	6	47	118	364	87	126	17	3	.396	.600	.298
2004	NY Yankees	155	601	112	172	24	2	36	106	308	80	131	28	4	.375	.512	.286
Career Totals		1430	5590	1121	1707	309	24	381	1096	3207	639	1126	205	50	.381	.574	.305

— Cumulative Post Season Hitting —

SEASON	TEAM	G	AB	R	H	2B	3B	HR	RBI	TB	BB	SO	SB	CSO	BP	SLG	AVG
1995	Seattle Mariners	2	2	1	0	0	0	0	0	0	0	1	0	0	.000	.000	.000
1997	Seattle Mariners	4	16	1	5	1	0	1	1	9	0	5	0	0	.313	.563	.313
2000	Seattle Mariners	9	35	4	13	2	0	2	7	21	3	10	1	1	.421	.600	.371
2004	NY Yankees	11	50	11	16	5	0	3	8	30	6	7	2	1	.414	.600	.320
Career Totals		26	103	17	34	8	0	6	16	60	9	23	3	0	.395	.583	.330

– All-Star Hitting –

SEASON	TEAM	G	AB	R	H	2B	3B	HR	RBI	TB	BB	SO	SB	CS	OBP	SLG	AVG
1996	American League	1	1	0	0	0	0	0	0	0	0	0	0	0	0	.000	.000
1997	American League	1	3	0	1	0	0	0	0	1	0	2	0	0	0	.333	.333
1998	American League	1	3	2	2	0	0	1	1	5	0	1	0	0	0	1.667	.667
2001	American League	1	2	0	0	0	0	0	0	0	0	2	0	0	.000	.000	.000
2002	American League	1	2	0	0	0	0	0	0	0	0	2	0	0	.000	.000	.000
2003	American League	1	3	1	1	0	0	0	0	1	0	1	0	0	.333	.333	.333
2004	American League	1	3	0	1	0	1	0	1	3	0	1	0	0	.333	1.000	.333
Career Totals		7	17	3	5	0	1	1	2	10	0	9	0	0	0	.588	.294

– Fielding –

SEASON	TEAM	POS	G	GS	INN	TC	PO	A	E	DP	FPCT
1994	Seattle Mariners	SS	17	17	142.0	71	20	45	6	9	.915
1995	Seattle Mariners	SS	46	38	342.0	170	56	106	8	14	.953
1996	Seattle Mariners	SS	146	145	1267.0	657	238	404	15	92	.977
1997	Seattle Mariners	SS	140	140	1233.0	627	209	394	24	83	.962
1998	Seattle Mariners	SS	160	160	1138.0	731	268	445	18	90	.975
1999	Seattle Mariners	SS	129	129	1116.0	614	216	384	14	105	.977
2000	Seattle Mariners	SS	148	148	1285.0	693	243	440	10	123	.986
2001	Texas Rangers	SS	161	161	1395.1	750	280	452	18	118	.976
2002	Texas Rangers	SS	162	160	1390.2	741	259	472	10	108	.987
2003	Texas Rangers	SS	158	158	1369.2	699	227	464	8	111	.989
2004	NY Yankees	3B	155	155	1364.1	375	100	262	13	25	.965
2004	NY Yankees	SS	2	0	2.0	2	1	1	0	1	1.000
Career Totals			1424	1412	11045.0	6130	2117	3869	144	879	.977